EARLY BRITISH HISTORY

Changes in Britain from the Stone Age to the Iron Age

Claire Throp

Raintree is an imprint of Capstone Global Library Limited, a company incorporated in England and Wales having its registered office at 7 Pilgrim Street, London, EC4V 6LB – Registered company number: 6695582

www.raintree.co.uk
myorders@raintree.co.uk

Edited by Helen Cox-Cannons and Holly Beaumont
Designed by Richard Parker
Original illustrations © Capstone Global Library Limited 2015
Illustrated by Martin Sanders (Beehive Illustration)
Picture research by Svetlana Zhurkin and Pam Mitsakos
Production by Helen McCreath
Originated by Capstone Global Library Limited
Printed and bound in China by CTPS

ISBN 978 1 406 29106 3 (hardback)
18 17 16 15 14
10 9 8 7 6 5 4 3 2 1

ISBN 978 1 406 29111 7 (paperback)
19 18 17 16 15
10 9 8 7 6 5 4 3 2 1

British Library Cataloguing in Publication Data
A full catalogue record for this book is available from the British Library.

Acknowledgements
We would like to thank the following for permission to reproduce photographs: Bridgeman Images: Ashmolean Museum, University of Oxford, UK, 23; agefotostock: CM Dixon, 5; Alamy: Doug Blane, 8, Jeff Morgan 01, 9, Jim Nicholson, 4, lowefoto, 20, Robert Morris, 27, Skyscan Photolibrary, 26, Steve Speller, 17, Wild Places Photography/Chris Howes, 14, 15; Corbis: Loop Images/Chris Warren, 24; Getty Images: UIG/Universal History Archive, 18; iStockphotos: hmproudlove, 11; Newscom: Robert Harding/Adam Woolfitt, 22, Robert Harding/David Lomax, 21, World History Archive, 29; Shutterstock: ADA_photo, cover inset (arrowhead), Capture Light, 13, David Woods, 28, Gail Johnson, 12, Hyena Reality, background (throughout), jaroslava V, 16, Jule_Berlin, 10, Karramba Production, cover (top left), back cover, Marcx1978, cover inset (hand axe), Matthew Jacques, cover, Stanislav Petrov, background (throughout), TTphoto, 25, Vadim Sadovski, 6—7 (back); Wikipedia: Portable Antiquities Scheme, 19.

We would like to thank Dr Mark Zumbuhl of the University of Oxford for his invaluable help in the preparation of this book.

Every effort has been made to contact copyright holders of material reproduced in this book. Any omissions will be rectified in subsequent printings if notice is given to the publisher.

All the internet addresses (URLs) given in this book were valid at the time of going to press. However, due to the dynamic nature of the internet, some addresses may have changed, or sites may have changed or ceased to exist since publication. While the author and publisher regret any inconvenience this may cause readers, no responsibility for any such changes can be accepted by either the author or the publisher.

Contents

Some words in this book appear in bold, **like this.** You can find out what they mean by looking in the glossary.

The first settlers in Britain

Humans have been living in Britain for hundreds of thousands of years. We know this because tools made out of **flint** from at least 840,000 years ago have been found at Happisburgh (pronounced "haze-bruh") in Norfolk. It had been thought that northern Europe was too cold for people at that time, but these tools have shown this was not the case. People did not live here all the time, though. It was much later — 12000 BC — before people began to live in Britain **permanently**.

CRESWELL CRAGS

This cave art at Church Hole Cave, part of Creswell Crags in Nottinghamshire, is probably about 13,000 years old. It shows animals including birds and deer.

These ancient flint blades were found at Star Carr in Yorkshire.

Hunter-gatherers

Early peoples were hunter-gatherers and killed animals for food using tools made from bone, stone and wood. They often pushed animals off cliffs or into bogs so that they were easier to kill. Sometimes they took meat from animals that were already dead. However, they did not kill animals just for meat. They also used the animals' skins for clothing and for shelters.

Britain was once connected to what is now northern Europe until sea levels rose so high that the country became an island, in around 6100 BC. The human population at this time was tiny.

TIMELINE

The Stone Age to the Iron Age period in Britain covers many years. It is difficult to give exact dates because it was so long ago. The dates of some of the events in this timeline are guesses based on what historians and **archaeologists** have discovered.

> For an explanation of what AD and BC mean, please see the glossary on page 30.

At least 840,000 years ago
The first tools are made in what is now Norfolk

About 14,000 years ago
The first **permanent** settlers live in Britain

9000 BC
Groups of hunter-gatherers live across Britain

around 6100 BC
Britain becomes an island. Before this time, the land was attached to northern Europe.

The Stone Age (4000 BC to 2500 BC)

4000 BC
Farming begins in Britain

4000 BC
Flint mines are first dug at Cissbury, Sussex

3000 BC
Work starts on Stonehenge

3200–2500 BC
People live in the village of Skara Brae, Orkney

The Bronze Age (2500 BC to 800 BC)

2500 BC
People begin to make tools from metal

1860 BC
The Great Orme copper mine is in use from this time

The Iron Age (800 BC to AD 43)

800 BC
People begin to make weapons from a new metal called iron

450 BC
People begin to live in more **permanent settlements**

The Stone Age

The Stone Age lasted for thousands of years. In this book, we take a look at the later Stone Age, from about 4000 BC – or 6,000 years ago.

ARCHAEOLOGISTS

We have very little written information about what happened in Britain before the Romans settled here in AD 43. The only way we can find out about what happened is to use archaeology. **Archaeologists** dig for objects from the past. They use these objects to find out more about people or places from long ago.

Early farmers

In 4000 BC, much of Britain was covered with forests. People used fire to clear the forests for land where they could keep animals. Wheat and barley were grown for food. A steady supply of food allowed people to stay in an area for longer, so **settlements** began to appear.

Flint

Many of the tools found from the Stone Age are made from a rock called **flint**. Finding flint was obviously important for people who needed it to make weapons and cutting tools. Flint mining took place in Cissbury, Sussex, from around 4000 BC. A few hundred tunnels have been found underground. Miners only had deer antlers and bones to mine the flint. About 1,000 years later, people dug for flint at Grimes Graves in Norfolk. Around 400 pits were dug there. The mines were 9 metres deep in places.

These actors are demonstrating flint knapping. Knapping was the way flint tools were made, by striking and chipping them into shape.

Homes

Skara Brae, in the Orkney Islands of Scotland, is a **settlement** of eight houses from around 3200 BC. The single-roomed houses are made from sandstone. Each house was linked to the others by passageways.

The people who lived at Skara Brae would have had only basic tools made from sandstone or animal bones. This means that the building of homes, and later the stone circles (for example, Brodgar), showed that it was a proper **community**. Many people would have had to work together over a long time to build these places.

The last people left Skara Brae around 2200 BC. No one knows why.

SKARA BRAE

We know about Skara Brae only because a huge storm in 1850 battered the Bay of Skaill. It blew away the sand and revealed the first stones of Skara Brae's buildings.

There was very little wood available at Skara Brae, so much of the furniture, such as this dresser, was made from stone.

Life at Skara Brae

About 50–100 people lived at Skara Brae. It is thought that they fished for fish and shellfish, grew barley and wheat, and kept sheep and cattle. They had stone beds that would have been made more comfortable with layers of plants and animal skins. Pottery could be displayed on stone dressers. Decorated jars, pottery and bone bead necklaces have all been found at Skara Brae. There were also dice for playing games. No weapons were found so it is likely that they lived in a peaceful time.

Other buildings

From about 3700 BC, long **barrow tombs** were built for burying the dead. They were usually rectangular, covered in earth and surrounded by a **ditch**. Some long barrows were multi-chambered. This meant that up to 50 people could be buried there. Long **cairns** were similar but covered in stones rather than earth. It seems likely that these tombs were used over many years.

BRYN CELLI DDU

Bryn Celli Ddu is a burial chamber on the Welsh island of Anglesey. Its name means "the mound in a dark grove". The chamber was built around 3000 BC. It is known as a passage tomb, a type of long barrow.

Castlerigg at Keswick (now in Cumbria) is one of the earliest stone circles in Britain. It dates from around 3000 BC. It has 38 standing stones, but there were probably more than that when it was first built.

Henges

About 5,000 years ago, people began to build **henges**. A henge is a ditch and a bank surrounding a circular area. Upright stones or large pieces of wood placed in the ground might also be found in the circle. Other stones were placed horizontally on top, such as at Avebury, Wiltshire, which was built 2850–2200 BC. Henges may have been built for religious ceremonies or to celebrate the seasons. Or they may have been gathering places for **trade**. Nobody knows for certain.

Early Bronze Age

There is no clear date when the Stone Age ended and the Bronze Age began. It was a gradual change. The Early Bronze Age is sometimes known as the Copper Age because so many things were made of copper at this time. However, many tools and weapons were still made of **flint**.

GREAT ORME MINE

The Great Orme mine in Llandudno, Wales, produced many tonnes of copper during the Bronze Age. **Archaeologists** have found nearly 6.5 kilometres of tunnels that date from between 1860 and 600 BC. It is thought that more than 10 million axes could have been made from the copper mined here and tin that was brought from Cornwall.

The Bell Beaker culture

Around 2500 BC, the Bell Beaker culture – named for the shape of the pottery it produced – came to Britain. Nobody knows whether people moved here and brought new metalworking **techniques** – particularly using gold and bronze – with them, or whether these developments came from people already living in Britain.

This stone hammer was used underground to help mine copper.

Making bronze

Gradually people worked out how to make bronze from copper and tin. Bronze is much stronger, lasts longer and is easier to shape than either tin or copper, so it was better for making tools and weapons.

Stone circles

The Early Bronze Age saw many stone circles being built. Perhaps the best-known stone circle is Stonehenge. It was built in several stages. About 3000 BC, Stonehenge was just a circular **ditch** surrounded by earth banks, with 56 pits inside the bank. The second stage of building Stonehenge happened around 2500 BC when the stones were placed in the centre. The smaller bluestones are thought to have come from Wales and the larger Sarsen stones from the Marlborough Downs.

Stonehenge, shown here, is on Salisbury Plain in Wiltshire, England.

TRADE

Trading with other countries began to take place in the Early Bronze Age. We know this because gold cups found under round barrows in southern Britain are very similar to those of the Mycenae in Greece.

Round barrows

A new type of **tomb** began to appear around 2000 BC. Round **barrows** were circular mounds of earth usually surrounded by a ditch and covering one or more bodies. **Grave goods**, such as pottery, necklaces and daggers, were buried alongside the bodies. **Cremation** — the burning of a body after death — became more common in the Late Bronze Age. The ashes of the body were placed in a pot called an urn and buried. Burial mounds in Scotland were sometimes covered in stones, as at the Nether Largie **cairns**.

It is unlikely that everyone was buried in the same way, though. The burial places we can see today, from long barrows to round barrows, might have been for the more important people in a **settlement**.

Ivinghoe Beacon in Buckinghamshire, England, is an example of a round barrow.

Middle and Late Bronze Age

The first larger **settlements** and farms, such as those found by **archaeologists** on Dartmoor and in Wales, appeared in the Middle Bronze Age. Walled fields were becoming common, to mark out land for growing food and feeding animals.

Jewellery and clothes

During this time it became very fashionable to wear jewellery. Bronze jewellery was sometimes made in styles found only in certain areas, such as the Sussex loop bracelet. This style has nearly always been found near Brighton, Sussex.

Gold rings, like these ones, were common in the middle or late Bronze Age.

THE LEWES HOARD

A hoard is a collection of valuable items such as coins, jewellery and weapons. A Middle Bronze Age hoard found near Lewes in Sussex in 2011 is more than 3,000 years old. Seventy-nine objects were found, including a jar containing pieces of jewellery, three axe heads and some objects that came from Europe.

Pottery

By this time, pottery dishes were being made in different sizes, probably because food was being prepared and cooked in different ways. There was more use of cereals, such as wheat.

Clothmaking

Metalworkers were clearly very skilled at this time, but other workers would have been improving their skills too. The reason we know so little about other skills is that materials such as wood and cloth rot away over time, whereas metal does not. Making cloth became more common in the Late Bronze Age. Men and women began to wear woollen clothing such as skirts and cloaks.

Flag Fen

Flag Fen causeway runs across the Fens, a marshy area of land in Norfolk and Cambridgeshire. Changes in the weather over time meant that this land was flooded by the Middle Bronze Age. Farmers had to move their farms to higher ground. The causeway, or raised path, was built around 1300 BC. People used it to walk across the flooded land, but a form of **ancestor worship** also took place there. When someone died, objects that were important to that person, such as weapons, were hidden between the posts of the causeway. People could return at any time to reconnect with their dead ancestors.

This is a reproduction of Flag Fen causeway. The causeway was made of 250,000 planks of wood and 60,000 wooden posts.

The remains of 24 houses from the Late Bronze Age or Early Iron Age have been found at Grimspound on Dartmoor.

Open spaces

By the end of the Bronze Age, the way people's lives were organized had changed. People lived in larger **settlements** and farming using a field system was commonplace. There were more open spaces, and fewer monuments, such as stone circles, were built. Burial mounds were less common because the land was needed for growing food. The dead were **cremated** and buried in urns near stone circles (because this was sacred land), or in flat graves near settlements.

The Iron Age

As with the change from the Stone Age to the Bronze Age, the change to making objects from iron rather than bronze was a gradual one. Bronze objects were made alongside iron ones for some time. Often bronze was used to make jewellery and iron to make weapons.

This decorated bronze shield dates from the Iron Age. It was discovered in the River Thames at Battersea in London.

THE CELTS

Today, people who lived during the Iron Age are often called Celts. They were not one group of people, however. Iron Age people did speak Celtic languages and have similar customs, but they lived in many different groups, or **tribes**.

Farming

New foods such as beans were grown, and in some areas land was set aside for animals to graze on grass. Farming **techniques** improved. Iron was used for axe heads and blades for the new, heavy ploughs. Some people think these ploughs were brought to Britain by Celts from Gaul (now known as France). The heavier ploughs were better for turning hard earth, although they needed more animals to pull them. Ploughs allowed farmers to grow more food in less time.

Many farms were only big enough to produce food for one family. The grain would have been stored in pits. They would have used any extra to **trade** for things they couldn't produce themselves.

Roundhouses

Many Iron Age people lived on farms or in roundhouses in villages. Roundhouses were made of wattle and daub. Wattle is made of hazel or willow twigs woven together. Daub is a mixture of mud, animal poo and straw. The houses would have been dark inside because there were no windows. Smoke from a central fire would have escaped through the thatched roof, made of straw or reeds. Houses in the north would have been made of stone and clay.

These roundhouses at Castell Henllys in Pembrokeshire, Wales, have been recreated.

Brochs

A broch is a circular stone tower, and there are about 500 of them in Scotland. Usually they would stand alone, but in the Orkney Islands they were often linked with villages. The Broch of Gurness was built between 500 and 200 BC. The main family of the village would probably have lived in the broch, which would have had several floors, with a spiral staircase leading between them. About 40 other families are thought to have lived in the village.

Hill forts

There are 3,000 hill forts across Britain, mainly in the south and west of the country. Most were built during the Iron Age, although some appeared in the Late Bronze Age. Hill forts were built on the top of a hill and surrounded by ramparts at the bottom of the hill. Ramparts are high walls with a walkway along the top.

Mousa Broch, in the Shetland Islands in Scotland, stands over 13 metres high and is perhaps the best surviving example of a broch in Britain.

Settlements

It is thought that there were different uses for hill forts around the country and over time. At first they were small and used as meeting places for **trade** or **worship**. Some were used for defence. Later hill forts, such as Danebury in Hampshire, were **permanent settlements**. **Archaeologists** believe that 300–400 people lived at Danebury in 73 roundhouses.

MAIDEN CASTLE

Maiden Castle in Dorset is a hill fort that was built in the early Iron Age. Although it started as a small **community**, in the later Iron Age many people lived there in roundhouses built in rows. Grain was stored in pits dug into the ground. Metalworkers and cloth workers are known to have lived at Maiden Castle.

Danebury hill fort is thought to have been built about 2,500 years ago.

Tribes

The **tribes** in Britain often fought with each other, so there were probably attacks made on forts of rival kingdoms. This is possibly why large ramparts were built around places like Maiden Castle. They were used to help protect the castle from outside attacks. Other hill forts were abandoned around this time. Larger, defended settlements called oppida began to appear in southern Britain from the 1st or 2nd century BC. Many people lived in these settlements and they were probably seen as important places.

Huge changes

Britain changed a great deal from the Stone Age to the Iron Age. People went from living as hunter-gatherers to living in **permanent settlements** and forming **tribes**. Farming **techniques** improved. Styles of monuments changed, particularly the way people buried their dead.

The Ring of Brodgar in the Orkney Islands was built at the end of the Stone Age.

From making tools and weapons out of **flint** in the Stone Age, people developed the skills to make stronger, longer-lasting objects from bronze and iron. Decoration of jewellery and other metal objects became more complicated, showing what great skills the metalworkers had developed.

Snettisham hoard

While we know quite a lot about the Stone, Bronze and Iron Ages in Britain, much of people's lives then remain a mystery. A hoard found in the ground in Snettisham in Norfolk includes some of the best metalwork ever discovered in Britain. Coins, bracelets and twisted metal neck rings called torcs were found, and most were made of gold or silver. The coins have helped **archaeologists** to date the hoard to about 70 BC. What we don't know, however, is why the hoard was there. Was it to keep the objects safe? Or was it part of a religious **offering**? Nobody knows.

This torc neck ring is made from a mixture of gold and silver. The person who wore it would have been very important.

The Romans

The Celtic tribes continued to fight amongst each other. Then, in 55 BC, the Roman Army invaded. The invasion was unsuccessful, but it was not long before they tried again.

Glossary

AD dates after the birth of Christ; these count upwards so AD 20 is earlier than AD 25

ancestor person who lived before us a long time ago

archaeologist person who studies places and objects from the past

barrow large mound of earth, built to mark where a person was buried

BC dates before the birth of Christ; these count downwards, so 25 BC is earlier than 20 BC

cairn pile of stones that marks a place where someone was buried. Cairns can also mark where a battle took place, or the direction of a path.

community group of people living in the same area and with something in common

cremation the burning of a dead body. The remains were usually kept in an urn.

ditch narrow channel dug into the ground, usually to hold water

flint type of hard stone found in the ground

grave goods objects that were buried in graves alongside the dead bodies

henge type of monument that included a circle of upright stones or pieces of wood surrounded by a ditch or bank of earth

offering something given to please a god or goddess

permanently all the time

settlement place where people make their homes

technique way of doing something, such as making bronze weapons

tomb place where a dead person is buried

trade buying and selling goods

tribe group of people with the same language, beliefs and customs

worship take part in a religious ceremony

Find out more

Books

Life in the Stone Age, Bronze Age and Iron Age (A Child's History of Britain), Anita Ganeri (Raintree, 2014)

Stone Age to Iron Age (History Detective Investigates), Clare Hibbert (Wayland, 2014)

The Secrets of Stonehenge, Mick Manning (Frances Lincoln, 2013)

Websites

www.bbc.co.uk/history/handsonhistory/ancient-britain.shtml
Learn more about ancient Britain on this BBC website.

www.bbc.co.uk/wales/celts
This website has animated stories to help you learn about Iron Age Britain.

www.yac-uk.org/timeline/ironage
If you are interested in archaeology then try the Young Archaeologists' Club. Members' ages range from age 8 to 17.

Places to visit

If you want to visit some of the places in this book, such as Stonehenge, find out more at the following websites:

The National Trust in England, Wales and Northern Ireland
www.nationaltrust.org.uk

The National Trust in Scotland
www.nts.org.uk/Home

English Heritage
www.english-heritage.org.uk

Index